SEEDED AND SODDED

SEEDED AND SODDED

THOUGHTS FROM A GARDENING LIFE

CAROL J. MICHEL

Gardenangelist Books

Copyright (c) 2019 Carol Michel

Published by Gardenangelist Books

Indianapolis, Indiana

All rights reserved. No part of this book may be reproduced in any form or by any means without the prior written permission of the publisher, excepting brief quotations in connections with reviews written specifically for inclusion in magazines or newspapers, or limited excerpts strictly for personal use.

Editor: Deb Wiley
Managing Editor: Katie Elzer-Peters
Copy Editor: Billie Brownell
Designer: Nathan Bauer

ISBN-13: 978-0-9986979-8-7

Printed in the United States of America

For my siblings, who let me be the one who planted peas in the spring.

Contents

CHAPTER 1
How My Obsession Began 5

CHAPTER 2
How to Make Your Garden a Humongous Success 9

CHAPTER 3
What Percent Gardener Are You? 13

CHAPTER 4
Advance Scouts 17

CHAPTER 5
Killing Is for Weeds 21

CHAPTER 6
Gardening with a GPS 25

CHAPTER 7
Gloriosa Vanderhort and Other Gardening Friends 29

CHAPTER 8
Dr. Hortfreud 33

CHAPTER 9
The Perfect Plant Deserves a Waltz 35

CHAPTER 10
The Pauli Exclusion Principle As It Relates to Gardening 39

CHAPTER 11
Plantoverts 41

CHAPTER 12
Gardeners? Superstitious? 43

CHAPTER 13
Hortotropism 45

CHAPTER 14
I Feel Like a Movie Star 47

CHAPTER 15
A Letter to My Lawn 49

CHAPTER 16
Society of Gardeners Aged 50 and Over 53

CHAPTER 17
In Search of Plants That No Longer Exist 57

CHAPTER 18
Pusley 61

CHAPTER 19
GUTS 63

CHAPTER 20
The Rewards of a Garden 65

CHAPTER 21
Garden Excellence or Garden Success? 67

CHAPTER 22
Failure Is on the Menu 71

CHAPTER 23
Garden-Colored Glasses 73

CHAPTER 24
Helicopter Gardening 75

CHAPTER 25
The Wilderness Called 77

CHAPTER 26
Haughtyculturist 81

CHAPTER 27
Chief Gardening Officer 85

CHAPTER 28
She Saw Me: A Chipmunk's Tale 89

CHAPTER 29
Hortombobulated 93

CHAPTER 30
The Perfect Plant Variety Name 97

CHAPTER 31
The Mystery of Plastic Pots 99

CHAPTER 32
The Optimist and the Pessimist 101

CHAPTER 33
Lettuce and Thistle 105

CHAPTER 34
The Old Woman at the Door 107

CHAPTER 35
If You Want To Change Your World 111

CHAPTER 36
Is Gardening Worth It? 113

Acknowledgments 115

About the Author 119

More Information 121

CHAPTER 1

HOW MY OBSESSION BEGAN

One of the great mysteries of life is how, among a set of siblings, one sibling can become obsessed with gardening, and the others go on to lead relatively normal lives. How does that *happen?*

Did one of the siblings just happen to breathe in some kind of magical pollen as a child that set her on the path toward becoming an eccentric gardener? Maybe she once cut herself while gardening and some chlorophyll mixed in with her blood and coursed through her veins, compelling her to forever want to garden? Or was she kidnapped by garden fairies, brainwashed, and then returned home?

Perhaps I should offer my own siblings—three sisters and a brother—and me as a case study should anyone be interested in trying to figure out what happened decades ago when we were kids growing up in a Midwestern suburb. What caused one of us to become so obsessed with gardening that one day she would even start writing a new thing called a "blog" and make it about gardening *(www.maydreamsgardens.com)*? What would cause her to collect many of those online musings into a trilogy of books, one of which happens to be the one you are reading now?

As I recall—and not all my siblings have the same recollection—we each had equal opportunities to help my dad in the garden. He never discouraged any of us from helping to plant peas in early spring or go with him out to a friend's farm to bag up some well-rotted horse manure to bring home to fertilize the tomato plants. Trips like that one taught us a lot about the hard work of gardening as we helped shovel the manure into trash bags and then rode home with our heads hanging out the windows, trying to catch a breath of fresh air instead of the aroma that followed those bags. My dad told us that the horse manure and all those other country odors smelled like money.

It took me years to figure out what he meant when he said that.

If helping to bring home trash bags filled with horse manure didn't knock any desire to garden clean out of us, the resulting invasion of millipedes that took over our backyard that summer at least gave us pause as we stood at the back door deciding if we should brave the onslaught to go outside. The millipedes, which we assume came from the horse manure, lived up to their name in many ways. There were millions of them *everywhere*, or so it seemed. On the patio, the picnic table, the lawn furniture. Everywhere. You could not step or sit anywhere in the backyard without first swiping away the millipedes.

Eventually, Mother Nature conquered the millipedes

or, at least greatly reduced the population to something less apocalyptic, and the next summer life in the garden more or less returned to normal. I suspect at that point my siblings decided to go on to other pursuits, but I headed right back out to the garden where I learned to sow seeds, plant seedlings, stake tomato plants, and trim shrubs in typical 1970s fashion.

Over the next several decades between then and now, I've continued to forge ahead of my siblings, and pretty much every other kid who grew up in my neighborhood, in my pursuit of gardening, rarely deterred by bugs or anything else Mother Nature throws at me, including a few terrible droughts, a couple of tree-breaking ice storms, and populations of Japanese beetles that made those millipedes seem like a blessing.

Nothing keeps me from gardening. Just ask my siblings.

And nothing keeps me from writing about it. Just ask anyone.

CHAPTER 2

HOW TO MAKE YOUR GARDEN A HUMONGOUS SUCCESS

If I stand in my garden on what is a relatively quiet morning, I can hear humming all around me. There's the hum of an interstate, which I never thought was that close to my house but which is close enough to hear the hum of traffic as cars and trucks zip around the city.

Sometimes I hear the hum of air conditioners, especially on the hottest summer days when only foolish gardeners and mad dogs are out and about. Everyone else is inside listening to the hum of their refrigerators.

On nice Saturday mornings and sometimes in the evenings, I hear the hum of lawnmowers. Then I, without thinking, look down at my own lawn to see if I should mow it even if I mowed it the day before or earlier in the day. There is just something about that kind of humming that makes me want to get out my own mower and join in the chorus.

So you won't be surprised to learn that I think things that "hum" are important to gardening.

First, every garden needs a little *hum*or because

sometimes we just have to laugh at what goes on in the garden. Maybe the humor comes from an odd flower combination we never expected. A vine that grows the opposite direction we intended it to grow. A newly dug potato that looks like Winnie the Pooh. Or two carrots entwined in an embrace that makes us blush when we see it.

Next, every garden needs a little *hum*ility because a good garden ought to *hum*ble a gardener a little bit. We get all swell-headed over some exotic flower we've finally managed to grow after years of trying. Then the next day we visit the garden of a less-experienced gardener, and they've got that same exotic flower growing everywhere like it's some kind of weed. Nothing humbles us more, unless perhaps it is the failure of an easy-to-grow annual flower like a marigold or a can't-miss zucchini squash that *should* provide us with enough food for the entire neighborhood. When they fail, and sometimes they do, we must swallow our gardening pride, slink off to the farmers market, and buy what we need there.

Every garden needs a little *hum*us, too, because we all know it is soil with humus that makes the biggest difference in a garden. We can try to garden without good soil full of rich humus, but it is much better to garden with it. Plants grow better, birds sing louder, and crickets jump higher when the soil is good. And the gardener smiles a lot more too.

Right now, perhaps you are thinking, "Hmmm ... she's right. Every garden needs a little hum. A little *hum*or, a little *hum*ility, and a little *hum*us to make it a *hum*ongous success."

If so, great! Now you can easily ignore those other hums of highways and lawnmowers and air conditioners. You can stop thinking, "Bah, *hum*bug!" when the weather is foul or Mother Nature fails to cooperate and follow your plan.

You are on your way to making your garden a HUMONGOUS success.

CHAPTER 3

WHAT PERCENT GARDENER ARE YOU?

More and more people are spitting into a little tube, mailing that tube filled with their spittle to a DNA lab, and then eagerly awaiting a report to show them, by percentages, from where their ancestors most likely came. But does that knowledge help them know how much of a gardener they are? Probably not.

That's why I've come up with a method anyone can use to find out what percent gardener they are, and it doesn't involve spitting, mailing, or waiting. All you have to do is review a few statements and rate yourself based on how closely the statement describes you. If you are unsure, ask a close friend or family member to rate you. And, of course, you can rate other relatives too.

Give yourself 10 points if the statement exactly describes you. Give yourself 5 points if you think it doesn't describe you now, but it could someday. Give yourself 0 points if it doesn't describe you at all and never will.

- You think a pleasant day is one that ends with dirt

under your fingernails, mud on your jeans, a green stain across your forehead, and a big grin on your face. In other words, a day you've spent gardening.
- Whenever you go to a big box store, you always head straight to the gardening section, even in the middle of winter when it consists of a few gardening tools marked down to get them out of the way to make room for more holiday decorations.
- You receive more than ten seed catalogs in the mail each year. Yes, bulb catalogs count too.
- Your personal library looks like a home for lost gardening books, with gardening books on all the shelves and overflow gardening books teetering in piles by your favorite reading chair.
- When you are with friends and someone sees a flower they don't know the name of, they automatically ask you what it is called, and you know the name. If you don't know the name, you are determined to find out.
- If the owners of your local greenhouse don't see you on their opening day in the spring, they call you to see if you are sick. You are also friends with them on Facebook. If you don't have a local greenhouse, you can give yourself max points if you regularly drive 25 miles or more to go to a garden center.
- You plan your vacations around visiting gardens.
- You belong to at least one garden club, plant society, or other horticulturally related organization.
- No one leaves your garden without a passalong plant.

- You are proud to be called the crazy gardening lady (or guy) of your neighborhood.

Review your score: 10 points for every statement that describes you, 5 points for any statement you think could describe you, and 0 points for any statement that doesn't describe you at all.

Add up your points; it will be a number between 0 to 100. *That's* what percent gardener you are!

CHAPTER 4

ADVANCE SCOUTS

Rising up above the foliage of the perennials in a garden border, two flowers showed up early in a garden.

The two blooms, conspicuous among the leaves, looked as though they were advance scouts, checking out the garden to see if it would be safe to bloom there.

"What do you think, Purple Flower, or can I call you PF?"

"I'm not sure what I think, but aren't those some other flowers over there across the green sea, Lovely Bloom, or can I call you LB?"

"Yes, please do. I think, based on the color, those other flowers aren't from our family. We are in the Aster family. If I'm not mistaken, those are members of the Rose family clear over there."

"I think you're right, LB. I've heard they are thorny, so we'd better stay here, lest we get stuck by them."

"PF, in case you hadn't noticed, we are rooted here; we aren't going anywhere."

"Oh, right, LB. I almost forgot. We are definitely not

tumbleweeds. They can at least roll to other places."

"We are a lot better looking than tumbleweeds, too, PF. Do you think anyone will notice how we bloom from the top down rather than the bottom up like most other flower spikes?"

"I hope so. It makes us unique."

"And we are native flowers. This is our homeland. Anyway, what were we supposed to be doing, PF? Oh, right. We are scouting out this garden to see if others in our family might want to bloom here. So far, it looks pretty nice."

"I did see a rabbit hop down that path behind us, LB, but then right after it came a gardener. That's a good sign, that there's a gardener here. I'd hate to wake up in the morning and find a rabbit nibbling on my lower leaves. I shudder to think of something so ghastly."

"Oh, don't flatter yourself, PF. I don't think that rabbit would like your lower leaves. Yes, it is good to see a gardener here, but I wish she'd weed that path behind us. Or is it in front of us? Anyway, there are all kinds of tree seedlings in it. She needs to weed it."

"I agree, LB, she definitely has some work to do in that path. You can tell her."

"Me? I'm a flower. Flowers don't talk, although I've heard there is a language of flowers. Anyway, we don't talk, PF."

"Oh, right. So how are we communicating now, LB, if this isn't talking?"

"Beats me. Anyway, this looks like a good garden, and we are the first blooms here in this border. Let's tell the others. We are going to be so pretty here."

"Hey, is that a bee, LB? It is a bee! I'm so excited. A bee. Am I old enough to know about bees?"

"Yes, PF, if you are old enough to bloom, you are old enough to know about bees. Now be still and maybe a nice bee will come along and ... oops, I can't say any more. Gotta keep this book clean. Anyway, let's tell the others to bloom now too!"

CHAPTER 5

KILLING IS FOR WEEDS

I've never killed a plant I purposely planted in my garden. But, sadly, sometimes plants die on me, either for an inexplicable or explicable reason. I do cringe a little when the reason is explicable, but it doesn't mean I killed it.

Perhaps I put the plant in a less-than-ideal location, expecting a plant that likes wet feet to adapt to dry conditions or vice versa. Or maybe I planted two opposites—a plant that likes it dry and a plant that likes it wet—side by side and then tried to compromise on the watering, resulting in one plant begging for a life jacket to keep from drowning and the other plant holding up its empty glass, unable to speak on its own behalf because it was so parched.

I imagine at one point those two unlikely plant neighbors looked at each another, clasped their stems together, and, like the last passengers on the sinking *Titanic*, accepted their inevitable fate and died.

But I didn't kill them.

Every once in a while, my pruners slip or I make an ill-advised jab with my dandelion digger and cut off a little plant, which then may not come back from its roots. I didn't kill it, though, because it is not *my* fault if it doesn't recover from its beheading and dies instead. It should have learned from the weeds how to recover from being cut off. No self-respecting plant with the name "weed" ever dies just because we cut it off.

Sometimes I accidentally cover up a plant, perhaps after zealously mulching the garden or by putting a stepping stone over a dormant plant because it was dormant and hiding, and I had forgotten it was there. *And* the plant dies. But I didn't kill it any more than Dorothy Gale killed the Wicked Witch of the West when Dorothy's house fell on her in the movie *The Wizard of Oz*. As I recall from watching that movie when I was a kid, Dorothy was quite appalled at the idea that she killed the witch. *Her* house killed the witch! Poor, confused Dorothy had no control over where her house landed when it was picked up by that tornado. With that same logic, I feel confident in saying a gardener cannot always stop something or someone from accidentally covering up a plant in her garden, killing the plant.

Sometimes I optimistically put a sun-loving plant in a shady location that I thought got enough sun. I may have been stretching the definition of "enough sun," especially since it was a favorite spot where normally only moss grew. I offer my optimism as my defense, my belief that plants want to live and don't need ideal conditions to do so. Therefore, *I* didn't kill the plant; I was merely misinformed on its overall willingness to survive in less-than-ideal conditions.

On a few occasions, by which I mean more occasions than a nongardener could ever understand, I've dismissed a plant from my garden. I changed my mind about it. Perhaps it got bigger than it should have. Or it had a bad habit of self-sowing that no one warned me about. Or it could be that it was always in my way when I walked around a particularly tight corner of the garden. Or it slashed me one too many times with its thorns. Yes, I'll admit it. I have fallen in love with roses, planted them, and then later decided those thorns must go, and summarily dismissed those roses from my garden.

Or maybe a plant just needed to go because we'd grown apart, and I had taken up with a new plant that would be perfect right where that other plant was. This reason in particular for dismissing a plant is hard to explain to a nongardener who doesn't necessarily see each plant in a garden as a unique individual, the way gardeners do. The nongardener sees a plant merely as some stems with leaves that add to the overall green of the garden. To them, one plant is as good as the next, or rather, as green as another.

No matter the reason, once I've dismissed a plant from my garden, which on more than one occasion also required me to emotionally distance myself from that plant, I either waited until it died, or I dug it out, cut it out, tore it out, plucked it out, or grubbed it out. But *I never outright killed that plant.*

Killing is for weeds and weeds alone. Every gardener knows weeds will never disappear on their own, never wither from our neglect, never stop growing regardless of the amount of water, light, or dirt they are actually growing in. No. They must die by a gardener's hands, which implies, of course, that we must kill them.

To the uninformed, the methods by which we gardeners kill weeds look quite a bit like the methods we employ to dismiss a plant we've grown tired of. We dig those weeds out, tear them out, cut them back, pluck them out, or grub them out. We slay them. They are weeds. *They must die!* Everyone understands this, yet no one puts the chlorophyll of these plants on the gardener's hands.

But when it comes to the plants we no longer want in our gardens, I refuse to accept that we gardeners kill them. We bid them farewell, we thank them, we explain why they simply cannot stay in the garden. We may even try to find new homes for them in other gardens. At the very least, we apologize to them right before we sever their roots. But we don't kill them.

Because killing is for weeds.

CHAPTER 6

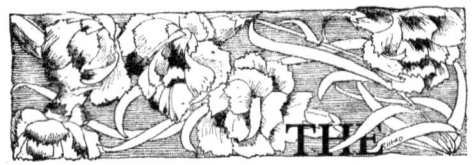

GARDENING WITH A GPS

Some gardeners might like a GPS, a *garden positioning system*, to tell them exactly which plants to grow and where to grow them to reach their goal of having a nice garden. They want instructions, even if they really do know what they are doing in their gardens.

What if there really were a GPS for gardening?

If I used a GPS to plant my garden, it would go something like this:

Me: Please provide plans for a vegetable garden.
GPS: *Calculating requirements for a vegetable garden. Proceed to a sunny spot in the yard.*

I would dutifully follow those instructions because a vegetable garden does like a sunny spot. But after that?

GPS: *Plant a tomato plant.*

I'd grab a packet of zinnia seeds to add some color to the garden.

GPS: *Put down those zinnia seeds; this is a vegetable garden. Plant a tomato plant.*

I'd defiantly sow those zinnia seeds and then grab a handful of green bean seeds.

GPS: *Recalculating garden plan. Sow green bean seeds in a long, straight row.*

Ha! I'd plant those beans, but I'd plant them in short, straight rows.

GPS: *Sigh. Recalculating garden plan. Plant tomato plants.*

Oh, really? I'd proceed with planting marigolds next.

GPS: *Pull out those marigold plants at your next opportunity.*

Nope, not going to do that.

GPS: *Recalculating garden plan. Plant tomato plants.*

The GPS at this point would begin to sound a bit frantic, so I'd go ahead and plant tomatoes, hoping if I followed one of its instructions, it might calm down and proceed to the next step.

GPS: *Proceed to plant pepper plants.*

You bet! But instead of planting pepper plants next, I'd add some nasturtium flowers.

GPS: *Recalculating veggie garden plan again. Legally plant pepper plants at your next opportunity.*

Back and forth we'd go. Me doing whatever I wanted to do. The GPS constantly recalculating the garden plan. Then, when I had finished all the planting, I'd survey my garden. I'd be happy with how it turned out, with the journey I took to get it to look how I wanted it to look.

In the background, using the last of its battery power, the beleaguered GPS would proudly announce, "*You have planted a vegetable garden,*" forgetting that it had little to do with how my garden actually turned out.

And thus, I would prove you do not need a GPS, or anything else, to provide step-by-step instructions for planting your garden. Follow your instincts, plant what you love, and you'll enjoy your garden far more in the long run.

CHAPTER 7

GLORIOSA VANDERHORT AND OTHER GARDENING FRIENDS

Do you dread getting your credit card statements after the Christmas holidays? Ha! You should see my credit card statements after the month of May. By early June, those statements often look like a complete directory of nursery and garden centers around my side of town and beyond. Some garden centers are even listed more than once.

I have to give some credit (or blame) to my garden stylist, Gloriosa Vanderhort. She has expensive tastes and often whispers in my ear, "You work hard to earn your money. What else are you going to spend it on? When will you ever see that plant again? When will you be here again where they are selling these garden sculptures? You want your garden to be pretty and stylish, don't you? Now is the time."

Then Ms. Hortefeller, my other garden center-visiting companion, takes over. She marches me up to the cash register, pulls out my credit card, and buys the plants and everything else like she has the money of a Rockefeller.

Once Ms. Vanderhort and Ms. Hortefeller get done

shopping, I feel like I need to turn to that tightwad gardener in all of us, Ms. Hortwad, to restore balance and save up for the next big garden shopping spree in the fall. But I try to leave Ms. Hortwad at home when I am actually at the garden centers. She can be a real downer with her concern about budgets and having money to buy food and gas and pay the mortgage.

The list of my amiable gardening companions includes more than Ms. Vanderhort, Ms. Hortefeller, and Ms. Hortwad.

If I am need of analysis, I can head out to my garden for a long session with Dr. Hortfreud. I am her primary patient and source of amusement.

Her esteemed colleague is the great scientist and experimenter, Dr. Hortenstein. As far as I know, Dr. Hortenstein's experiments, which usually involve me trying something new in the garden, have so far been fairly harmless. At least I haven't noticed unexplainable creatures peeking out from behind garden fences, or crawling under gates, or lying in wait under a shrub.

Just for fun, and because it makes Dr. Hortfreud shake her head in wonder, I sometimes consult the Great Hortini, a magician and fortune teller when it comes to matters of the garden. So far, she has been no more accurate than an almanac in forecasting the weather each year.

There are others!

HortGreenhouse is the auditing firm responsible for reviewing the finances of my garden, and if I were to hand out awards, I would have them make sure any voting was on the up and up.

F. Lee Hortley takes care of legal matters.

Mysteries of the garden, such as the location of lost gardening tools and gloves, are handled by the detectives Hortcule Poirot and Hortlock Holmes. As far as I know, they haven't had to solve a murder mystery, though there was a time when I found a dead meadow vole after clearing the driveway of snow one clear winter day. I swear it was an accident. Deputy Sheriff Horty Fife did not press charges.

Does it end there? Maybe for now. The great Hortocrates, a philosopher of gardening, thinks it should.

CHAPTER 8

DR. HORTFREUD

What do you call the voice in your head that talks to you while you are out in your garden? Dr. Hortfreud, of course.

Hello, Carol!

Hi, Dr. Hortfreud.

I see that you've come out to the garden for a final session this fall.

Yes, I mowed the lawn today, probably for the last time this season.

That's good. Now let's begin this session with a little word association. I'll say a word or phrase and you say the first thing that comes to mind. Are you ready?

I guess so.

Okay. First word is "frosting."

What is on the leaves after the first frost.

Not cake? Okay, let's try another word. "Short."

What the lawn should be going into winter.

I see. How about "winter?"

A good time for a gardener to rest up for spring.

Interesting. Let's mix it up a bit. "Catalog."
Seeds.
I'm starting to see a definite trend here. How about "TV"?
There are not enough gardening shows on TV.
Let's try one more word. "Inside."
Houseplants.
Are you ever not thinking about the garden and plants?
Is that a rhetorical question, Dr. Hortfreud, or do you really want an answer?
I'm not sure yet. Let's try a few more words. "Music."
The sound of cicadas in late summer with the buzz of bees in the background.
Sigh. Before I admit defeat, I'm going to try one more word. "Basketball."
A sport that is played mostly in winter, making it a great activity for gardeners to watch because it doesn't take too much time away from the garden.
That's it. I'm ending our session now. I can't think of any words you couldn't relate to gardening. Apparently your brain is hardwired so everything relates to gardening. Or might I say, gardening is rooted pretty deep in you!

CHAPTER 9

THE PERFECT PLANT DESERVES A WALTZ

Every gardener soon learns how to do the waltz in the garden. It begins innocently enough with a trip to the garden center, perhaps just to buy a few bags of topsoil or mulch. We tell ourselves we won't look at the plants. There's no time, really, and the garden is already full of plants.

Then we arrive at the garden center, perhaps at the same time as a new shipment of plants or maybe just after all the watering has been done, and so the plants look fresh and eager and oh so pretty.

As we scurry through the garden center to get to the potting soil, we are thinking about how we will not look at the plants, we will not look at the plants, WE WILL NOT LOOK AT THE PLANTS ... and then we see it.

Our eyes might lock in on a particularly striking bloom or our heart jumps at some variegated foliage. We move closer. We check the tag. We lose our willpower, our objective thinking. We will buy that plant. But do we have a place to plant it?

Such a question is too practical to ask or even answer at this point. It is too nice a plant to pass up. We've never seen one like it before. We will rationalize about all the many places it could go, or if no spot comes to mind, we'll convince ourselves that we will find a place to plant it once we get it home. Or maybe we'll tell that little white lie we all tell ourselves, that it will be no trouble at all to dig up a new border, just a small one, so the new plant has a new home where it can be a focal point.

We do what we have to do. We buy the plant and take it home, perhaps forgetting about the mulch or whatever reason we had for going to the garden center in the first place.

And then we begin the waltz in the garden.

We carry the new plant from place to place in the garden, looking for the perfect spot to plant it. It may be a short waltz, if we find the right location quickly. Or the waltz may turn into a wild polka if we find the perfect spot, but see it is occupied by another plant. Then we switch our plant dancing partners and dance with that other plant and maybe several more plants in succession to make space for our new plant.

Then the actual planting part of the dance begins. We set the plant down, twirl it this way and spin it that way in do-si-do fashion until we are satisfied that, indeed, it is in the right spot, and we have the best side of the plant facing the way we want it.

We dig a nice hole, perhaps with a trowel for a small perennial plant, or maybe with a shovel if we had the nerve to ask a tree to dance the waltz without knowing exactly where we might plant it. And then the waltz concludes with a *pat, pat, pat* as we tamp the soil gently around the base of the plant and water it in.

Having done well with this dance, we are eager to find the next partner, the next plant, ready for a new dance to begin.

CHAPTER 10

THE PAULI EXCLUSION PRINCIPLE AS IT RELATES TO GARDENING

Dear Hortense Hoelove,
How does the Pauli Exclusion Principle relate to gardening?
Signed,
Carol

Dear Carol,

I am so glad you didn't ask, "Does the Pauli Exclusion Principle relate to gardening?" because then I would have had to answer *yes* and move on. How one asks a question can make such a big difference. Thankfully, you asked "how," so I shall tell you how the Pauli Exclusion Principle relates to gardening.

For us ordinary gardeners, the Pauli Exclusion Principle, a real principle developed by a theoretical physicist named Wolfgang Pauli, essentially means two solid objects cannot be in the same place at the same time.

How is this relevant to gardening? Well, let us assume

that plants are solid objects. Yes, of course I know that many plants have lots of limbs spread far enough apart that birds and butterflies can fly through them, but that doesn't mean that those limbs aren't solid. Therefore, this principle is relevant to gardening in that we should space our plants so that they are given enough room to grow without having to fight another plant for the same space.

When plants have to fight for the same space, one plant will lose and one will win. They simply can't occupy the same space at the same time. If they try to grow in the same space, the more vigorous grower will always win.

Time and time again, though, some gardeners place plants so close together that one wonders if they think this principle does not apply to their gardens. The arrogance! I suppose they are just so anxious for their gardens to look filled in that they forget to give the plants the space to grow into their own form. Please, if this is your problem, take into account the Pauli Exclusion Principle and give your plants their own space to grow.

On the other hand, if you are one of those gardeners who insists that each plant in your garden has its own space so that it dare not even touch leaves with the plants next to it, well, that is wrong too.

I think plants look best if they are allowed to intermingle. To hold limbs occasionally. To touch leaves. To live in another's shadow. But they cannot occupy the same exact space at the same time. After all, there are some principles we cannot ignore.

Sincerely,
Hortense

CHAPTER 11

PLANTOVERTS

At some point in life, someone will label us or we will label ourselves as either an introvert or an extrovert. If we seem to draw energy from being alone, we'll usually be called introverts. We think a lot without making a sound. If we seem to draw energy from being around other people, we'll be labeled extroverts. We probably think out loud.

But what if we draw energy from working in a garden, from being around plants? What if, after a day of sharpening all the edges of all the borders in the garden by hand-digging them, we are so tired and sore we can barely move, yet we feel quite energetic, alive with ideas and ambition to do more both in and out of the garden?

What if, after spending a few hours pulling out unwanted plants and replanting a garden border with new plants, we can't wait to come across another blank spot in the garden so we can continue planting?

What if, after a day in the garden, we feel like we have the energy to face the outside world once again, and we have the ability to solve any problem life sends our way?

What if we do our best thinking while in a garden? What label describes us then?

Plantovert.

Plantoverts draw more energy from plants and gardens than from being alone or being with people. They do their best thinking while gardening.

Plantoverts can also be either introverts or extroverts.

That would make some people introverted plantoverts. I bet they like to garden best in a back garden with a high fence all the way around it so they can garden mostly alone, undisturbed. Just them and their plants.

And some people might be extroverted plantoverts. I think they probably like to garden in their front garden where people can see them and stop to chat with them and ask them all kinds of questions about their gardens.

Of course, new words need official definitions.

---

plantovert

[plant-oh-vurt]

Noun

1. A person who draws energy from gardening or working around plants.

The plantoverts were always the first ones to arrive at the garden center in the spring. Carol is a plantovert who often spends time alone in her garden, tending not only plants but also ideas.

Maybe someday, plantovert will end up in an actual dictionary!

CHAPTER 12

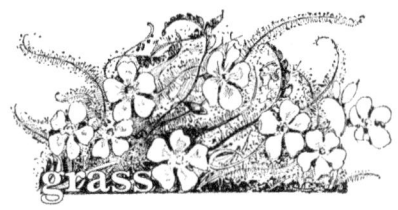

GARDENERS? SUPERSTITIOUS?

There are some superstitions about gardening that you might want to give some consideration to, just in case, because you never know—some of them might be rooted in some truth.

For example, everyone knows that a passalong plant won't grow if you thank the giver for it. Many of us also know from first-hand experience that it's hard *not* to say "thank you" when offered a free plant. After all, gardeners are generally friendly, gracious, and appreciative. But with practice, when you are given a free plant, you can instead say something like, "That will look good with my hostas" or "I have the perfect spot for that plant."

You can say anything you want, just don't say "thank you" when someone gives you a free plant.

Did you know that seeds grow when a pregnant woman plants them? This doesn't mean that you are pregnant if the seeds you sow grow, or that the seeds won't grow if you aren't pregnant. It just means, if you believe in this superstition, that perhaps having a pregnant woman sow the seeds in your garden makes it more likely that the seeds will germinate.

There are even superstitions related to hoes. "If you carry a hoe, spade, or shovel into the house, you must carry it out the same door you came in by, or a death will follow." Death? I've carried a hoe into my house plenty of times—who hasn't—but I must be carrying them out the same door I came in as there haven't been any deaths that I can relate to any hoe-carrying episodes on my part.

There is another superstition that if you do carry a hoe into your house, you have to walk backwards to carry it out to avoid bad luck. I refuse to believe this is true. I feel like I have lots of good luck, and I don't walk out backwards with my hoes. Maybe carrying more than one hoe in the house switches the luck from bad to good? I've done that a few times.

In fact, I say it is bad luck to own just one hoe. I'll just go on record and say the more hoes you own, the better your luck will be, and the fuller your life will be. And I have proof of this in my own garage where I have dozens of working hoes and at least a dozen old hoes whose best gardening days are behind them. I have hoes for every gardening condition and every type of gardener and a full gardening life to go with them.

As for all those gardening superstitions, you can follow them or not, but you might want to toss a bit of fertilizer over your left shoulder for good luck. Just in case.

CHAPTER 13

HORTOTROPISM

You won't find a definition for hortotropism in a dictionary, but that doesn't mean it doesn't exist. In fact, if you are a gardener and have more than once struck up a conversation with someone you didn't know who happened to be gardening nearby, you know that hortotropism does exist. It's that natural inclination by gardeners to start talking to one another about gardening.

In fact, and I can personally attest to this; most of us gardeners cannot resist talking to someone about gardening if we catch them in the act of planting or watering or otherwise tending a garden.

Sometimes we feel compelled to talk about the weather. Is it good for gardening? Been too dry? Too wet? Too cold? Too hot? Even if we aren't from the same climate, when we meet other gardeners, we compare notes on our weather differences. "I wish I had snow," the gardener from the South might say. "I wish I could garden outside in January," the gardener from the North might say.

We find after just a few minutes of talking that we speak a common language, one that even members of our own family don't speak if they don't garden. We talk about deadheading and hardiness zones. We compare notes on pruners and potting soil. We talk about the advantages of homegrown and handpicked vegetables. We speak in botanical nomenclature.

We have found kindred spirits! They understand us. We understand them, even though we may have met just five minutes earlier. We meet gardeners, we find new friends. That's hortotropism.

> hortotropism
> [hort-o-trop-ism]
>
> Noun
> 1. The natural attraction between two people once they both realize they are gardeners.
>
> *It was hortotropism that caused her to speak to the stranger planting petunias by the sidewalk.*

CHAPTER 14

I FEEL LIKE A MOVIE STAR

When I'm out in the garden, especially when I'm mowing the lawn, I feel like a movie star.

Sometimes I channel Sally Field in *Places in the Heart* when she played the part of Edna Spalding. In the movie, Edna, a young widow in Texas, had to take over the family farm after her husband died and harvest the cotton so she could pay the mortgage.

Remember those scenes when she is out in the fields picking cotton with her ragtag crew and her kids? Remember how sweaty she looked? That's how I look sometimes when I am mowing the lawn. All sweaty like that. Fortunately, though, I don't have to mow the lawn to pay the mortgage the way Edna had to pick the cotton so she could pay her mortgage.

Other times, I play the part of Rose Sayer, brought to the big screen by none other than Katharine Hepburn. Rose was a missionary somewhere in Africa whose brother was killed by the Germans in World War I. Rose then convinced a man named Charlie, played by Humphrey Bogart, who had a boat called the *African

Queen, to go after a German ship so they could blow it up to avenge the death of her brother. Katharine looked quite sweaty as they chugged along on that old boat, didn't she? I wonder if that was real sweat or fake Hollywood sweat?

Of course, I don't generally wear a frilly shirt with a high lace color and long sleeves like Katharine did in that movie. In weather like I experience in the summertime, I wear T-shirts and shorts and lather on the sunscreen lotion.

What I do share in common with Katharine in *The African Queen* is I wear a wide-brimmed hat, though my hat doesn't have a long chiffon ribbon to tie it on.

Then there are the times when I feel like the movie star Vivien Leigh when she played the part of Scarlett O'Hara in *Gone with the Wind,* especially the scene where Scarlett is out in the vegetable garden digging for root crops to eat, sweating like crazy, and swearing she'll never go hungry again. In that scene, she's wearing an old bonnet.

I wonder what the neighbors would think if I wore an old bonnet when I mowed the lawn or went out to the garden to dig up some carrots. Maybe I could complete the ensemble by making a dress out of curtains that were just hanging around?

No, I'd better not wear an elaborate dress while mowing. I'll stick to my shorts and T-shirts. But I'll always feel like a movie star, with real sweat, not fake sweat, every time I mow the lawn.

CHAPTER 15

A LETTER TO MY LAWN

Late Fall
My Dearest Lawn,

First, let me say you know how proud I am of you. From the beginning of spring, you were the first lawn on the street to really green up. I was happy to bring out the lawn mower and give you a good cut. Remember how sharp the blade was back then, after I had it professionally sharpened?

Through most of the spring, I never minded that I had to mow you every four or five days, really I didn't! We were exercising together, we were enjoying the fresh air and the sunshine. Even in the summer, because of Daylight Saving Time, I could mow later in the day and avoid all of that heat, making it easier to keep up our twice weekly time together. I was so happy and proud of how you looked in early summer.

And all summer, you never asked for extra water! You were content with whatever rain you got and never made me haul out all the hoses and sprinklers. Yes, there was that brief time in late August, early September when you really could have used some extra water, but you held on until the rains came again. I was so proud of you!

You still look great.

But I have to tell you, I am getting just a wee bit tired of all this mowing. Today I had to mow you again, and I had just cut you a few days before that. What is going on? Why are you demanding so much of my time so late in the season? Why are you so needy?

You knew you would get cut today, didn't you? The sky was blue, the sun was shining, it was a perfect 72 degrees Fahrenheit, and you had grown so much in just two days. Then when I read that the weatherman thought it might start raining tomorrow, you knew you had me, and that I would mow you.

I didn't let you down, did I?

But enough is enough. You need to start slowing down and put some more energy into your roots and not the blades of grass. Really! It's autumn now. I can't keep up this schedule. I've got other things to do, other plants to tend to, garden chores that must be done before the snow flies. So I wouldn't mind, well, I'd really like it, if you would at least slow down enough so I only have to mow you once a week until you are done around Thanksgiving.

Now, don't be upset. I am proud of you, really I am, and I think you are by far the best lawn in the neighborhood, the envy of all. And I know you probably can't help yourself with this rain and cooler temperatures, which you so love. But please think about next season this winter.

You've really got to stop growing so much!

Sincerely,
The one who mows you

CHAPTER 16

SOCIETY OF GARDENERS AGED 50 AND OVER

Dear Membership Committee Chairperson,

Please consider this letter my official application for membership in the Society of Gardeners Aged 50 and Over (SGAFO).

I have worked, studied, and planned my entire life to be admitted to this society and I now humbly, but excitedly, present myself before the membership committee on my fiftieth birthday, asking for your consideration of my qualifications, which include:

An interest in all things horticultural, including plants, gardens, gardening tools, and gardening books.

A lifetime of gardening experience, beginning at age two when, according to family legend, I dipped my hands into a bag of fertilizer, which caused my mother to have to call poison control, and continuing through the years as I gained decades of actual hands-on gardening experience in all seasons.

A gardening wardrobe that includes an old-lady wide-brimmed hat for protection from the sun and four pairs of gardening clogs, bought and worn long before similar footwear became popular with nongardeners. I have a keen sense of garden fashion, attired mostly in green tops and pants that are big enough not to split open when I lean over to pull weeds.

An active membership in an actual garden club.

A learned ability not to scream like a little girl and run the other way when encountering insects, spiders, and snakes in the garden. Instead, I look them squarely in the eyes and determine if they are friend or foe. If foe, I willingly fight the battle against them, even with my bare hands. If friend, I leave them be.

A noticeable increase in the use of the phrase "I remember when" when discussing matters of gardening, such as, "I remember when my dad bought tomato plants at a bait-and-tackle store because there were no garden centers in town." Or, "I remember when I was studying horticulture in college, we didn't have the internet to look up information on plants." Or, "I remember when I took ownership of my dad's night-blooming cereus houseplant back in '87; how I looked forward to it blooming under my watch."

I've also become very adept with sentences that start with "Back when" as in, "Back when I was a kid gardening." "Back when we thought a white marigold was a miracle to behold." "Back when everyone had a vegetable garden in their backyard."

An appreciation for the finer gifts of gardening,

including compost, rocks, and topsoil.

In addition to these qualifications, I can provide several letters of recommendation from family and friends, both gardening and nongardening, attesting to my interest and practice of gardening.

I can also provide a copy of my birth certificate, should you find it hard to believe that someone as young as I am is actually qualified to be in your wonderful organization, the Society of Gardeners Aged 50 and Over.

Let me close by saying I have the greatest respect and admiration for all current and past members of this wonderful society, for their plant knowledge and growing experience, and for their tenacity and sense of purpose when it comes to gardening. I would be pleased to be counted as one of them. In fact, I am resolved to garden even more so that I might be considered for the high honor of sitting at the table with elder gardeners for many more decades.

Thank you for your consideration. If there is anything I've missed about being an elder gardener, please let me know.

Yours truly,
Carol, May Dreams Gardens

CHAPTER 17

IN SEARCH OF PLANTS THAT NO LONGER EXIST

Obsessed gardener looking for an old variety of *Begonia*, 'Gloire de Lorraine'.

As described by Buckner Hollingsworth in *Gardening on Main Street* (1968):

"*From a tight cushion of bright green foliage a great many lax stems emerged, each tipped with only two flowers, but when these fade and fall, the stem lengthens and two more flowers appear. There are so many stems of so many varying lengths that the plant becomes a fountain of rose-colored flowers.*"

Hollingsworth also called it by another common name, "A Yard of Roses."

I wanted it.

I searched the internet and found a reference to the begonia 'Gloire de Lorraine' in a place called the past, in an issue of *American Gardening* dated December 1, 1900.

I found another article about 'Gloire de Lorraine'

dated 1968, the same year *Gardening on Main Street* was published. And I quote:

> "The decline in popularity of Gloire de Lorraine Begonias can be chiefly attributed to their unsatisfactory response to the living room climate. The leaves tend to curl and turn yellowish, and usually sooner or later become attacked by mildew which rapidly renders the plant unsightly. Moreover, the plants are susceptible to bud drop, and the flower colour presents only a limited range: white or light to deep pink."

I still wanted it.

Someone who went by the initials H.G.L. wrote the editor of *Country Life in America* back in 1903, "*anxious to learn the secret of success in this culture*" of Begonia 'Gloire de Lorraine'. He had lost nearly all his begonias and wanted to know how to save those he had left. The editor provided a lengthy answer describing when the begonia needs a period of rest, how to harden it off so the buds don't drop when the plant is inside, and more. He made it seem just a bit challenging to keep this plant going from year to year.

At this point, a more rational gardener might have given up looking for this begonia.

I still wanted it.

But I don't think I'm going to get it. I think it really is in the past. Gone forever.

This is one of the pitfalls of reading old gardening books. They often describe plants that are lost to the ages, cast aside in favor of newer, maybe better, varieties or hybrids. I could find newer, maybe better, begonias that long ago replaced 'Gloire de Lorraine'. I'm not sure I want them. I just want to grow the begonia Hollingsworth described. Or at least, try.

I'll keep advertising.

Obsessed gardener looking for an old variety of Begonia, 'Gloire de Lorraine'.

Someday, maybe, I'll find it.

CHAPTER 18

PUSLEY

I went out to the garden one day to check on my green beans and sweet corn, saying a little prayer as I walked out to the vegetable garden that I wouldn't find the tender seedlings eaten to nubbins by rabbits. As I approached the garden, I saw with horror that my problem wasn't rabbits this time, it was a weed!

That darn purslane! Do rabbits bother to eat it? I don't think so! It is the bane of my vegetable gardening existence, and a source of constant annoyance and exasperation because it is nearly impossible to get rid of it.

If you hoe it under, every tiny piece of stem will grow a new plant. If you pull it and leave even a microscopic cell or two of a root behind, it seems it will grow back! Yes, it is edible and full of nutrients, but I have not personally tried eating it. And even if I did eat it, I could never eat as much as my garden is capable of growing if I turn my back on it even for a week.

A few years ago, I read *My Summer in a Garden*, written by Charles Dudley Warner in 1871, and he had this to say about purslane, or as he called it, pusley:

> "I scarcely dare trust myself to speak of the weeds. They grow as if the devil is in them. ... The sort of weed that I most hate (if I can be said to hate anything which grows in my own garden) is the "pusley," a fat, ground-clinging, spreading, greasy thing, and the most propagatious (it is not my fault if the word is not in the dictionary) plant I know. ... I am satisfied that it is useless to try to cultivate "pusley." I set a little of it to one side, and give it some extra care. It did not thrive as well as that which I was fighting. The fact is, there is a spirit of moral perversity in the plant, which makes it grow the more, the more it is interfered with. I am satisfied with that. I doubt if any one has raised more "pusley" this year than I have; and my warfare with it has been continual. Neither of us has slept much. If you combat it, it will grow, to use an expression that will be understood by many, like the devil."

At least purslane is not a new weed recently imported from a foreign country. Misery loves company, even if that company is over a hundred years old.

However, knowing that purslane, or if you prefer, pusley, has been a perverse weed for so many decades doesn't diminish the angst I feel when it takes over my own garden!

CHAPTER 19

GUTS

Maybe it is my background in information technology, where acronyms are made up faster than weeds spring up in a new garden, that made me think of the GUTS we need to garden.

It takes guts to **G**arden **U**nder **T**ough **S**ituations (GUTS). Wherever we garden, whether it is in hardiness zones on the edge of the Arctic Circle or in the middle of the Mojave Desert or some climate in between, there is something that seems to make it tough to grow what everyone else seems to be growing with ease.

Our soil can make for a tough situation. Perhaps it is a sticky, heavy, wet clay soil that clings to every garden tool it comes in contact with. Maybe our soil is made up of an abundance of rocks that a shovel can barely penetrate without jarring us with each attempt to dig.

Or maybe the tough situation is that we have to plant the garden on a steep hill. Or in a flat area that floods and takes forever to dry out in the spring. Maybe we have no ground at all and must be content to plant in containers on a patio or balcony.

Guts are required when you go without rain for

several weeks, or years for some gardeners, or have too many days of temperatures well above average. It's gut-wrenching to see how the plants adapt, or don't adapt, to a drought. In your gut you know that some plants will just simply have to be let go, to live or not live without your watering.

Often when two or more gardeners gather, the conversation turns to who has the most guts to GUTS. It's not a contest I want to win. I'd rather have good weather, good soil, and an overall good place to garden than have to tough it out and Garden Under Tough Situations.

CHAPTER 20

THE REWARDS OF A GARDEN

"I once had a sparrow alight upon my shoulder for a moment, while I was hoeing in a village garden, and I felt that I was more distinguished by that circumstance that I should have been by any epaulet I could have worn."
~ Henry David Thoreau

Like Thoreau, when I see a new kind of bird in my garden, I feel as though it has paid me and my garden a great compliment with its presence. It chose my garden! I must have done something right in my choice of trees and shrubs, bird feeders, and birdbaths.

When I spot a toad hiding in the damp shade beneath some big hosta leaves, I feel honored that he (or she) has chosen my garden to make its home. When I see a praying mantis sitting on the edge of a leaf, I feel like it is nodding at me, affirming that I am doing the right thing in my garden by not spraying pesticides at the first sign of an aphid or Japanese beetle.

The bees buzz their compliments, as well, on my

choice of flowers. When a tomato ripens, a flower blooms, or the tree leaves change to their autumn colors, I feel as though each has given me its own reward for the time I spent laboring in my garden.

When the rabbits dart out from the strawberry bed having dined on the ripe berries ... well, let's not carry this "rewards from nature" analogy too far.

Like Thoreau, most of us truly delight in *nature* being in our gardens. The presence of all the creatures makes us secretly, or perhaps overtly, proud of our gardens, happy to have spent the hours working in it, often in solitude, to make it a place where all of them—birds, toads, bees, spiders, insects, and yes, even rabbits, voles, snakes, and squirrels—delight in being.

If we were to wait for someone to come by and present us with an award for our garden, most of us would wait forever. Awards are few and far between and subject to the rules and interpretations of others. But when we plant a garden, a good garden, we've already received our award a hundred times over from all—both flora and fauna—who chose to dwell within it.

CHAPTER 21

GARDEN EXCELLENCE OR GARDEN SUCCESS?

I once read a quote by Dale Carnegie, and my thoughts turned to gardening. As they always do. Before you read the quote, take a minute to answer this question: Would you rather be an excellent gardener or a successful gardener?

I suspect most of us would like to be successful gardeners but how would that success be measured? If we chose to be an excellent gardener, how would we define what "excellence" is?

Dale Carnegie provides an answer that may influence those who chose "successful" to change their response to "excellent."

"Success bases our worth on a comparison with others.

Excellence gauges our value by measuring us against our own potential. Success grants its rewards to the few but is the dream of the multitudes. Excellence is available to all living things but is accepted by the few." ~ Dale Carnegie

We are all tempted to look over the garden fence into our neighbor's garden to compare our garden to theirs. Who has fewer weeds? Better flowers? Nicer shrubs? Taller trees?

But where do such comparisons lead? If we think that our own gardens are lacking, these comparisons can and often do lead to us thinking or making negative comments about the neighbor's garden and his or her gardening ability. "If I had the kind of time she has." "Well, if I spent that kind of money." "His flowers are nice, but he seems to have no sense of color."

Somehow getting caught up in these types of criticisms and put-downs is often how we justify our own level of success in the garden, whether we are truly successful or not.

But if we strive for excellence as a gardener—defined as reaching our own potential—comparisons to others and their gardens are no longer necessary. We can measure our excellence by how close we came to our own potential.

And what is our potential? Our potential as gardeners ebbs and flows depending on the time, resources, knowledge, and money we have to invest in the garden at any given time. These can all be influenced by our own health, the demands of family, the demands of work, and even the temperament of Mother Nature in a given season.

As our potential changes, so will our gardens, and so will our definition of excellence. When we strive for excellence, we no longer need to make comparisons to see if our garden is better than our neighbor's garden. We just need to look within ourselves and ask if our garden reflects our full potential as a gardener at that point in time. If we can do that—garden to the fullest potential that we have at a given time—then we can and should consider ourselves to be excellent gardeners.

And thank goodness there is enough space in the garden of life for everyone to be excellent.

CHAPTER 22

FAILURE IS ON THE MENU

Welcome to your own private garden restaurant, Mother Nature's Diner.

You arrive and plan to order beautiful flowers to feast your eyes upon, loamy soil that looks like chocolate cake mix, and the perfect amount of rain to wash it all down. While you are dining, you'd like a few sweet birds to whistle songs to listen to, dozens of pretty butterflies to amuse you as they flutter by, and a bonnet full of bees to entertain you as they buzz from flower to flower.

But Mother Nature is a sassy waitress in this private garden restaurant. She decides what you will actually get and cares not a bit about what you ordered. She secretly has some failure on the menu, and for no reason at all she will decide to dish it up for you.

And what does that big ol' dish of failure look like when Mother Nature serves it up in your garden? It looks a lot like plants that die unexpectedly, flowers that never bloom, and ground that is harder than a day-old piece of pie left out overnight. The only birds seem to be nasty old starlings, you can't find a butterfly to save your garden, and the bees sting you without a second thought.

But all is not lost! You know that you can still have a healthy, happy garden even with some failure served up on occasion.

You just have to understand a bit about your waitress, Mother Nature, and what she likes.

She likes good compost and actually helps make that. She also likes plant diversity and maybe a water feature. Make sure to have them in your garden, and Mother Nature might be a little nicer when it comes time to serve you your main course, and your dessert too.

Keep in mind Mother Nature does not like gardeners who don't at least try to meet her halfway, so do try to help and pull your weight in Mother Nature's Diner by doing some weeding, some deadheading, and some planning for plants that will live and thrive with the amount of water she decides you will get.

Mother Nature's Diner is not a place where you want to act all uppity, like you own the joint. Do that, maybe flash some money around like you can buy whatever you want, and Mother Nature, the waitress, will give you a bad table, make you wait longer than anyone else, then plop a big ol' plate of garden failure in front of you and charge you double.

Be humble, be respectful, be gracious, be helpful, be thankful, and leave a big tip. Mother Nature may still serve you some humble pie, some failure every once in a while just to be sure you know she's not to be trifled with, but mostly she'll also serve you a lot of success, and you'll have a happy, healthy garden as a result.

CHAPTER 23

GARDEN-COLORED GLASSES

I see the world through garden-colored glasses. All around me I notice plants and flowers, and I must have plants and flowers around me as well. I rarely walk by a plant without an impulse to touch it. When I see soil, I want to feel it and smell it.

I will go places I wouldn't normally go if someone dangles words and ideas in front of me that relate to gardening. If someone says simple phrases like, "There's a garden there," or "We might go by a garden center," or "I think the trees will be in bloom," then I'm jumping into the car, ready to go.

I see the world through garden-colored glasses.

I'm not the only one with this view, though as with real glasses, there are various prescriptions of garden-colored glasses. Some focus on tropicals, others, on trees. Some of the garden-colored glasses bring vegetable gardens into sharp focus while others have magnifying powers that allow the wearer to see miniature gardens.

Still other garden-colored glasses are almost like 3D glasses, with special powers to see beyond the garden to where the garden fairies live.

And some garden-colored glasses are like bifocals or trifocals with several types of lenses for those who view and love all kinds of gardening.

Some people start wearing their garden-colored glasses at a young age. I think I started wearing mine at the age of two. Others discover their garden-colored glasses when they are older. Either way, once someone looks through garden-colored glasses, the world is no longer the same.

And even though the garden-colored glasses sometimes make those of us who wear them look a bit odd or eccentric, we don't mind because what we see—a world full of plants and gardens—amazes us.

CHAPTER 24

HELICOPTER GARDENING

The tower has cleared you and your gardening helicopter for landing.

Are you constantly checking to see which plants need more water, less water, more sun, less sun, more shade, less shade? Do you inspect your plants daily to figure out if they should be pruned, deadheaded, staked, or shaped? Do you take a magnifying glass with you so you can see deep into the crevices of the bark of the trees or stare into the eyes of tiny insects? Is the local soil testing lab named in your honor because you have had every soil test imaginable performed for your garden?

If you are constantly checking and inspecting your garden, hovering over it looking for signs of trouble, then land that helicopter, turn off the rotors, and turn in your pilot's license.

Stop hovering! Stop worrying about your garden. Stop fussing over the plants.

You are probably driving yourself and everyone around you nuts. You need to learn that plants require far less attention than you are giving them. Leave them alone. Let them grow.

Oh sure, you have to pay extra attention to the little seedlings so they don't dry up before they even have a chance. Ditto the newly transplanted. And it is a good idea to walk through your garden occasionally to look for signs of trouble like bad bugs, weeds, plant diseases, and flopped-over plants.

But by and large, just let the garden grow. Fight back the wilderness, show the garden you are in charge, follow the laws of Mother Nature, and don't sink your fortune into the plants. If you do all that and stop hovering and worrying, you'll end up with a healthy garden, and you'll be healthier too.

"Tower, we have another helicopter gardener ready to land."

CHAPTER 25

THE WILDERNESS CALLED

What was your garden before it was a garden?

It was a wilderness.

If you did nothing in your garden, the weeds, trees, bugs, grasses, and animals would just go wild. Like a teenager whose parents have left him alone while they go on an extended vacation, the wilderness will invite everything wild to come on in if there is no one at home to tend the garden.

Few people look at a complete wilderness and think, "There's a garden." Sure, there can be a bit of wilderness in a garden, and probably should be, but it can't be the whole garden. That's the first lesson I learned about having a healthy garden. You have to remember that your garden was once a part of the wilderness and that wilderness wants your garden back.

The weeds want to grow in your garden in any bare spots they can find and even in places that aren't bare. They will grow in the cracks of a patio, in the sludge left in the gutter, and even in a half-empty bag of topsoil. And they aren't content to just grow. They also want to flower, produce seed, and then scatter their seeds throughout the garden to ensure future generations of weeds for as long as you are tending your garden.

The rabbits want to eat your garden, and so do squirrels, chipmunks, voles, raccoons, mice, birds, and, unfortunately for some, deer. All of these wild animals have an appetite not just for weeds but also for the most expensive, most difficult to find, most treasured plants that you have personally planted in the middle of the wilderness you have attempted to turn into a garden.

The bugs want to eat, sleep, and make merry in your garden too. And not just good bugs, which any gardener would welcome as a sign of a healthy garden, but all kinds of bad bugs too.

Once we accept that the wilderness is always there in the background, waiting for its chance to overtake our gardens, then we aren't surprised and frustrated when we leave our gardens for a week or so and return to find that the wilderness spent the time of our absence creeping back in, trying to take over.

We soon learn it is futile to try to completely remove the wilderness from our gardens. We should want some of it—birds, bees, bugs, even a few bunnies—because they are part of a healthy garden. But we should feel free to fight back against some of it, including the weeds, the damaging predators, and anything else that wants to take over the garden completely.

Finally, when we are out in our gardens slaying weeds and other garden demons, we should remember that fighting back against the wilderness taking over our gardens is not the same as fighting Mother Nature.

Trying to break the laws of nature is a futile exercise that will only lead to frustration and eventual failure.

But the wilderness, it can be tamed a bit. Knowing that a big part of gardening is taming the wilderness and accepting that we can never tame it completely is a giant step toward a healthy garden and gardener.

CHAPTER 26

HAUGHTYCULTURIST

"The haughtyculturist is a good name for the kind of person who is as terrified of growing last year's roses as is a woman of being seen in last year's hats." ~ Wilfrid Blunt.

Do you know any haughtyculturists? The kind of gardener who has to have the most current flower varieties and would actually prefer if they were the only gardener they knew who had those flowers? Maybe you know a gardener who won't accept any plant that doesn't have a certain pedigree or tag? Or you've heard of a gardener who doesn't grow vegetables, or if they did, only grows them in a little potager all fixed up like it belongs in the gardens of Versailles in France?

If I ever invite a haughtyculturist to my garden—as if I knowingly would—I suspect they would look at the woodland violets I let grow in the lawn, and wherever else they take a fancy to, and wonder at my poor weeding habits. Would it matter to them that violets always remind me of being a little girl again, picking violets for my mom and grandma in the spring?

A haughtyculturist might look at my vegetable garden at the end of the season when the tomato plants are all askew, the corn stalks are dried up, and the leftover green beans are rattling in their pods and think to themselves how thankful they are that they would never have such a mess to clean up in their garden. Would it matter to them how well I ate from my garden all summer? That the tomatoes tasted like warm sunshine, the corn was as sweet as sugar, and the green beans were so plentiful that they grew faster than I could pick them?

A haughtyculturist might look at the pot of red geraniums on my back patio and think I am foolish, or uninformed on the latest and greatest flowers, for growing such a common old-fashioned flower. They might also look around and notice that it doesn't exactly match some of the flowers I've planted in other containers. They would surely think of dozens of better flowers to fill those containers. Would it matter to them that I am slightly sentimental about red geraniums because my dad always grew red geraniums, and that my pot of them is a remembrance of him?

I am certainly happy that, so far, I don't know too many haughtyculturists. In fact, I can't think of any that I know personally. I suspect that anyone who starts out as a haughtyculturist at some point gets knocked down a peg or two in their own garden because Mother Nature is really in charge there. She treats all gardeners the same, sometimes with pleasant, sunny days, and sometimes with scary, awful storms. She doesn't care if you are a common gardener or a haughtyculturist. She knocks down fancy one-of-a-kind flowers just as easily as she does common flowers.

My advice is never come close to being a haughtyculturist and avoid them if you can. Grow and let grow when it comes to other gardeners. Grow what you love to grow and you'll end up a happyculturist, which is the best kind of gardener to be.

CHAPTER 27

CHIEF GARDENING OFFICER

Congratulations! You've worked hard to get to the top. You've paid your dues and sown your seeds and now you are the Chief Gardening Officer of your very own garden.

You are in charge. You are the one who makes the final decisions. You decide which row to hoe, which weed to pull, which flower to plant. The buck stops on your potting bench.

You are now the one who is responsible for achieving a healthy garden. It's a lot of responsibility, but you've trained your whole life to become the Chief Gardening Officer, the CGO.

Perhaps you were a garden apprentice as a child, forced to pull weeds or mow the lawn in the hot summer sun. You hated it, but the CGO back then said it would be good for you, it would teach you how to someday be the CGO in your own garden. You weren't so sure about that. You thought at the time that if having your own garden meant a lifetime of weeding and mowing, then maybe you didn't want to have a garden.

But somewhere along the way, you decided that you did want your own garden. To prepare yourself maybe you read books on gardening, memorized the botanical names of your favorite plants, or visited other gardens to observe them and those who worked in them.

All the while, you were thinking about what you would do when you finally reached the top of the compost pile and had your very own garden. And now you are the Chief Gardening Officer, and you've learned a few things.

You've learned that you don't have as much freedom in the garden as you had hoped. Who does? There may be family members—your own personal board of directors—who insist on reviewing budgets and plans, who want to come out to the garden to have a look-see and express an opinion. But that's okay, a necessary evil, as it were. It's still your garden.

You've learned that to make it your own garden, you should plant what you want to plant and remove plants that you don't like. If you acquired your garden through a merger or acquisition and someone else was once the CGO of your garden, you've learned that it is okay to overthrow their regime and build up your own empire because now it's your garden.

You've learned that sometimes you should hire consultants to help you in your garden—garden coaches, garden designers, even landscape architects—to give you advice or help with design or just be a sounding board for your own brilliant ideas of what to do with your garden.

However, as the CGO, you have the final say. If you don't like what they say, you can let them go and bring in others. You've also learned that you can hire help for the heavy lifting in the garden, even bring in someone else to mow and weed, if that's what you want to do. You're the CGO, after all. You can't be expected to do it all, all the time.

Yes, congratulations on your promotion. The nameplate on the garden shed door finally has your name on it: Chief Gardening Officer. *Carpe hortus!* Long live your garden!

Now, go out there and be the best Chief Gardening Officer your garden has ever had. Go out there and build up your empire. Build up your garden!

CHAPTER 28

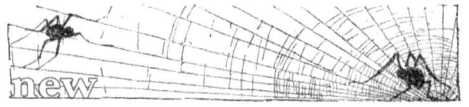

SHE SAW ME: A CHIPMUNK'S TALE

"She saw me!"

Chance Chipmunk was out of breath and soaking wet as his chipmunk friends and family gathered around to find out what happened.

"She saw me! And then she turned the hose on me and chased me as I ran and hid under the big hosta. She soaked me good."

"Oh dear," said Sweet Charlene Chipmunk. "Are you sure? Well, you are soaking wet. Maybe you fell in that birdbath again trying to get a drink of water after partying all night."

"No, I'm sure," said Chance. "She saw me, she chased me, she soaked me."

With that, everyone gasped and began to murmur among themselves. They were worried. What would the gardener do now that she knew there were chipmunks around her garden?

Some of them thought she would do nothing because she was so lazy. But the older, wiser chipmunks, including Charlemagne and Chadwick, shushed, yes shushed the crowd and began to lecture.

Everyone listened.

Charlemagne said, "We all need to be careful. It's possible she will set a trap with delicious food, and then when she catches you because you won't be able to resist the delicious food, she'll take you in the trap as far away as she can, usually across a body of water so you can't find your way back, and let you free there. If this happens to you, don't panic; there are other chipmunks on the other side of the water who will help you. In fact, our dear brother chipmunk, Chaucer, came to us that way. We took him in and he is one of us now."

With that, everyone around Chaucer patted him on the back to make sure he knew he was part of their family now.

Then Chadwick added, "Whatever you do, please do not get lured up any boards to find more delicious food like sunflower seeds. If you do that, it will lead you to a bucket of water, you'll fall in, and you'll drown, just like that."

They all shuddered at the thought.

Little Chester Chipmunk worked his way to the front of the group so he could be seen and heard and asked, "Does this mean we should stop eating her cherry tomatoes?"

Chadwick and Charlemagne conferred with each other and then made an announcement. "We think you can eat some of the cherry tomatoes because she never gets around to picking all of them but leave no trails of half-eaten fruit or she'll catch on to us."

"Should we worry about poisoned food?" asked Sweet Charlene Chipmunk.

"Heavens, no! This gardener would never poison us because she knows if one of us gets poisoned and dies out in the open, and then gets eaten by an owl or hawk, it will poison them too. No, we are safe from poisons."

Hearing there would be no threat of poisoning, they all relaxed a bit as tiny Chaplin Chipmunk came forward and announced, "I have a confession."

They all turned and looked at Chaplin.

"I got up on the front porch and dug in one of the containers there, and the gardener noticed. I'm sorry. I thought there was a delicious bug in there that I just had to eat. I was so hungry."

"Well, that's not good," said Chadwick. "But thank you for confessing. Now, everyone, listen up. We must all stay out of the containers. Nothing, I mean nothing, makes a gardener madder than finding out a chipmunk has been digging around in her containers. The gardener here is already not happy to have seen Chance. Now, repeat after me: No More Digging."

With that, they all chanted "No More Digging" in unison—Chance, Sweet Charlene, Charlemagne, Chadwick, Chaucer, Chester, tiny Chaplin, and all the other chipmunks—as they went their separate ways.

CHAPTER 29

HORTOMBOBULATED

"Hortombobulated."

If you know that the meaning of the word *discombobulated* is "to be thrown into confusion" and you are a gardener, you can readily comprehend that the meaning of the word hortombobulated is something along the lines of "to be thrown into confusion in a garden" or more precisely, "to be thrown into confusion on matters related to gardening."

For the record, I am not personally hortombobulated. Most of the time. I am not confused on matters related to gardening, though occasionally it looks as though I have no idea what I am doing in my garden, even after decades of gardening.

Sometimes in the spring it looks like I am darting about the garden with no sense of direction. Should I plant the vegetable garden first? What about those annual flowers I just bought? Do I have time to add some mulch? What if I just start this new flower bed over here? Is it time to mow yet? I think I need another trip to the garden center, perhaps for some more new flowers, to clear my mind.

Then in the fall, I repeat the drill, in reverse. Should I clear off the vegetable garden now? Or take out those annual flowers that now look nothing like the young, spry seedlings I bought months ago? I really must mulch or at least use up the mulch in those bags that have been sitting on the patio most of the summer. What about a new flower bed? And should I really leave all of this mess until spring? I think I need another trip to the garden center, perhaps for houseplants, to clear my mind.

Generally, most gardeners hoe themselves out of a hortombobulated state. They go out to their gardens and just start weeding, deadheading, pruning, mowing, sweating, and hoeing until they've worked everything out and feel less confused and more like their gardens are once again under control.

Other gardeners like to mow themselves from hortombobulation to hort-ease (you won't find either words in a dictionary—yet). Mowing the lawn gives the garden a sense of order, especially if the edges are nicely trimmed next to the flower beds that look anything but orderly.

I've even seen some gardeners try to shop their way out of their state of confusion by buying more plants, more seeds, more mulch, and better tools. It sounds like that would be the worst thing to do, but no garden center will turn you away when you arrive all crazed and wide-eyed in the spring, ready to buy.

For most cases of hortombobulation, it may be necessary to seek help, which can come from a family member or friend who is willing to lend a hand or hoe in the garden, under your direction, of course. For severe cases, I recommend consulting a garden designer, a garden coach, or some other qualified individual who can help you find the root cause of your hortombobulation.

Or be like me. Accept that spring and fall are times of high energy, high confusion, and much hortombobulation. Strap yourself into your wheelbarrow and enjoy the ride.

---

hortombobulated
[hort-um-bob-u-late-ed]

Adjective
1. To be thrown into a state of confusion on matters related to gardening.

Early in the spring, she was hortombulated, and they found her wandering in her garden wondering what to do first.

CHAPTER 30

THE PERFECT PLANT VARIETY NAME

The more I garden, the more I shake my head at some of the plant variety names breeders and marketers choose for new plants. I have every intention of remembering those names. I make valiant attempts to do so. I sometimes write the name of a new plant on a label and stick it around the base of the plant after planting it. Then I toss the label that came with the new plant into a big clay pot filled with other labels from other plants.

Then someone comes to visit me and my garden, and as we stroll by my new plant, we stop to admire it. Then my visitor asks, "What variety is that?" I reach down to find the label, and it is gone. Or I find the label but the writing on it has faded. And there isn't time to look through dozens of labels spilling out of a big clay pot full of labels to find the plant variety name.

Given all this, I think the perfect plant variety name is 'Missing Label'.

Just imagine the new scenario as you stroll through your garden with a friend and you both stop to admire a particularly lovely daylily. There are *thousands* of varieties of daylilies. Who can remember all their names? But this time you are ready because you know the variety name is the easy-to-remember 'Missing Label'.

"Oh, that's 'Missing Label,'" you could answer when your friend asks you what it is.

There are other good choices for plant variety names that are similar to 'Missing Label', including 'That Pretty One', 'Can't Remember', 'Given to Me by a Friend' (one of my favorites), and 'I Don't Know'.

But, clearly, the perfect plant variety name, the one that is most descriptive of so many plants in my garden, is 'Missing Label'.

CHAPTER 31

THE MYSTERY OF PLASTIC POTS

Plastic pots. Where do they all come from? It is a mystery yet to be solved. As spring continues, the first of the plastic pots filled with new plants begin to congregate on my front porch and the back patio, my two favorite plant-staging areas.

Once I get everything planted, I have towers of square and round, black and green plastic pots of all sizes. I have stacks of flats and piles of plant labels left behind. My first thought is I need to get rid of them as evidence because some people may be shocked at the number of pots I accumulated and think that it represents a lot of plants. They may wonder where I planted everything and what my gardening budget really is.

Let me set the record straight on behalf of all gardeners. We should draw no conclusions about the number of plants purchased based on the number of plastic pots left over. It is a mystery how there can be so many.

Every gardener knows that the empty pots make it look like we bought many more plants than we think we have bought. How else would you explain that, even though we may have dozens or hundreds of empty plastic pots, we still need more plants? Again, should anyone be looking for evidence of the number of plants a gardener has purchased, they should not try to count the leftover plastic pots.

It is like counting blades of grass to figure out how big a lawn is. It's an impossible task and the answer won't mean anything. In fact, what we should be doing is figuring out other causes for the accumulation of plastic pots in the spring. I have several theories including one involving garden fairies dragging pots to my house from the neighbors' garages and recycle bins.

I have also not yet ruled out the spontaneous replication of plastic pots, brought on by a process that involves sunlight and dirt. I'm still working out how that might happen.

I have doubts that I will eventually solve the mystery and find the cause for the number of plastic pots around my garden. In the meantime, let me repeat: I *do not* believe the number of plastic pots tells us anything about the number of plants purchased.

CHAPTER 32

THE OPTIMIST AND THE PESSIMIST

Two houseplants were sent out to the patio to spend the rest of the summer in plant rehab. We'll call one plant Purple Leaf and the other Ivy. Let's listen in as they discuss their situation.

Purple Leaf: Oh, look! Look! We are outside! Isn't it wonderful to see the sun like this and not through a window?

Ivy: Are you kidding me? I'm going to burn up out here. It's so bright. I want to go back inside. Who's in charge here?

Purple Leaf: Relax, Ivy. With all this nice sun we are sure to grow some big leaves now. I've noticed your leaves have been getting smaller lately. You could use some more chlorophyll.

Ivy: Well, okay. Maybe the extra sun will be nice, but geez, I'm drying up out here. We are going to need way more water than that sprinkling we get once a week inside, if we are lucky, that is.

Purple Leaf: Didn't you notice, Ivy? The plants out here get watered nearly every day.

Ivy: I knew it, I'm going to drown.

Purple Leaf: No, Ivy. You won't drown. You'll be just fine. Oh look, here she comes now with the water. I just love when I get watered so much it comes rushing out the bottom holes of my pot.

Ivy: Speaking of pots, I could use a new one here, and some new soil too. Do you know how long I've been in this container? And how old the soil is around my roots? It's been so long; it's just gross.

Purple Leaf: I think we are going to get new pots and new soil too. Look, there's a big bag of it over there. That has to be for us. I think I'd look wonderful in a dark green pot, don't you?

Ivy: If you say so. Hey, aren't we going to end up with a bunch of spiders and pillbugs moving in on us out here? Ick. Bugs. I hate bugs. I hate spiders too.

Purple Leaf: Relax. I'm sure she'll give us all new soil before we move back in later this fall. She doesn't want us to bring in bugs and spiders either. You really do need to stop worrying and relax. Please try to enjoy this outside treatment, Ivy.

Ivy: Fall? Did you say fall? We aren't going back inside until fall? That's kind of late for us to be out here, isn't it? What if there's an early frost and she's late bringing us inside. It will kill us. I need to go inside and lie down now. Help! Take me back inside!

Purple Leaf: Oh, for heaven's sake. Just stay put.

Ivy: Very funny, where do you think I'm going to go,

anyway? I'm as rooted as you are.

Purple Leaf: Well, then, be quiet. I'm trying to take advantage of this time outside to put out some new leaves. I mean, really, we are a sad couple of houseplants. We are so sad looking, the gardener won't take a picture of us. Instead, she took a picture of one of our neighboring plants, a canna, and put it someplace she called "online." Just look how pretty it is over there. Yoo-hoo, Canna! Over here! We are new here. Can you tell us when we'll get some fertilizer?

Ivy: Oh, I assumed we didn't get our pictures taken because of privacy laws. We are under treatment, after all, so she really shouldn't take our pictures. Though for the life of me, I cannot imagine why we are trusting her with our treatment. She's the one who has been so neglectful all these years.

Purple Leaf: Bygones! That was then and this is now, and isn't it a glorious day out here?

Ivy: If you like sun and all that, I guess it is. But isn't that a storm cloud over there?

Purple Leaf: Oh yes, and I love rainwater. It really is the best for our treatment, after all.

And so the summer continued with Ivy and Purple Leaf bantering back and forth. Eventually, Ivy calmed down and both were all too soon back inside, well before the first frost, and all the better for the time they spent in patio rehab.

CHAPTER 33

LETTUCE AND THISTLE

I sometimes think there are two gardeners tending my garden. Or possibly, one gardener with a split personality.

There is the Lettuce-Do-It-Gardener, who does things like sow seeds for morning glory vines. She's convinced that she'll somehow keep them from self-sowing all over the place.

And then there is the Thistle-Take-Some-Work-Gardener, who will have to spend hours weeding out morning glory vine seedlings while muttering about who thought sowing seeds for morning glories was a good idea.

Lettuce thought it was a good idea. Thistle will clean up the mess. They have quite the back-and-forth conversations.

"Lettuce order up 1,000 crocus corms to plant in the lawn this fall."
"Thistle take a lot of work to plant those 1,000 corms."
"Lettuce try to grow camellias!"

"Thistle be a disaster when we have to pull out those dead camellias."

"Lettuce plant some figs!"

"Thistle be a waste of time if we get frost before the fruit ripens."

"Lettuce make this garden border bigger!"

"Thistle take more time to weed and mulch."

Back and forth they go, Lettuce and Thistle. Thistle and Lettuce. Guess who usually gets her way? Lettuce think. Thistle be easy to figure out! Morning glory flowers are so pretty when the sunlight comes from behind and lights them up.

CHAPTER 34

THE OLD WOMAN AT THE DOOR

I was somewhat startled when I heard the doorbell ring and was tempted to ignore it. I wasn't expecting anyone, which meant it was probably someone who was going to invite me to their church or tell me about a candidate I simply had to vote for. Maybe it was a little kid selling candy or cookies? Why don't they ever sell plants door to door?

In spite of my instinct to just ignore whoever was there, I soon found myself opening the door and exchanging greetings with an old woman in a wide-brimmed hat wearing an old green sweatshirt and loose khaki pants with mud stains on the knees. She seemed delighted that I had opened the door, telling me that she had been looking for me and had a gardening secret to share.

At first I was suspicious. Who was this old woman? She seemed familiar to me, but I couldn't quite figure out why. I looked down at her feet and noticed she was wearing the same brand of gardening clogs that I wear, and her hat actually looked like the one I had been wearing for several years, though it appeared to be older and more worn out than mine.

There was something I immediately liked about this old woman, though don't ask me to describe that something because it would be difficult to put into words. I invited her in and she headed right for the sunroom, suggesting that we sit at the table in that room, and she would tell me the secret. As she walked toward the sunroom, she asked if I had any iced tea to drink. How did she know about the sunroom? Or that I would have iced tea in the refrigerator?

I went to the kitchen and dutifully poured some iced tea into two tall glasses, took them out to the sunroom, and sat across from the old woman. I noticed then that she had green eyes that were almost the color of mine, but a bit softer in color, perhaps a faded version of my own eyes. She took a sip of tea and paused.

Then, reaching across the table, she grabbed my hands, looked right at me, and said, "I've come to tell you a secret about gardening, one that many don't learn until it is nearly too late." I caught myself almost holding my breath as I waited for her to continue.

The old woman paused before speaking again. During that brief pause, I looked past her sitting across from me and out to my own garden. It was early in spring and I could see off in the distance a few yellow daffodils blooming in small clumps scattered here and there. The first hints of green looked like fuzzy halos around some of the trees. The vegetable garden was a blank slate, and I was eager to get out there and sow seeds for early spring crops.

With a soft clearing of her throat, the old woman once again captured my gaze and began to tell me her secret. "The secret I want you to know now, that many gardeners never figure out, is that no weed or insect or plant disease or weather calamity can do as much to prevent us from having the garden we want to have as procrastination can. If you rid your garden of procrastination, you'll have no regrets, and you'll have a garden that you can share with others because it won't be just in your mind, it will be a reality that you can sit in, stroll through, harvest from, and garden in."

She stopped speaking momentarily, giving me a few minutes to reflect on what she had said. I hastily made some notes so I could remember this secret exactly as she told it to me. Then she summed it up in just a few words: "Banish procrastination from your garden."

With those final words, she rose out of her chair and headed toward the door. As she crossed the threshold, she turned and said, "If it is okay with you, I'd like to come back occasionally to see how you are doing with your garden and perhaps share other secrets with you." I nodded yes and encouraged the old woman at the door to return whenever she wanted to.

With that assurance, she headed down the driveway

and disappeared around the corner. Before I could wonder how she got to my house, she was gone, and I suddenly could not wait to get out to the garden. I went back to my bedroom and changed into a comfortable pair of loose khaki pants with mud-stained knees and my favorite old green sweatshirt. On my way out, I grabbed my wide-brimmed hat and slipped on a pair of gardening clogs.

As I rounded up a hoe and a rake and headed back to the vegetable garden, I wondered if I would ever see the old woman at the door again. Somehow, I knew I would.

CHAPTER 35

IF YOU WANT TO CHANGE YOUR WORLD

If you want to change your world, plant a garden.

If you've already planted a garden, you know this is true. A garden gets you to go outside where you will come in contact with soil, which has amazing bacteria in it that improve your mood, if not your health.

A garden gets you to exercise, sometimes just a little bit, with a few knee squats as you do a bit of weeding, and sometimes quite a bit if you are toting bags of mulch or mowing the lawn.

A garden introduces you to beauty. A single flower. A perfect green bean. The way the sunlight filters through a tree canopy.

A garden provides you with sustenance if you choose to grow a bit of food. And why wouldn't you choose to grow a bit of food if given the opportunity? Is there any better vegetable than the one you grew yourself from a seed or a small seedling that you yourself planted?

A garden can erase your troubles and worries, sometimes for just a little while as you dig and weed and plant and harvest. But that little while can give you new perspectives, new insights, even better answers.

A garden can introduce you to other people who are also interested in gardening. And everyone knows a gardener introduced to another gardener has made an instant friend.

And a garden can connect you to the world, through the common experience shared by people around the world as they plant, tend, and harvest wherever they are.

If you want to change your world, plant a garden.

CHAPTER 36

IS GARDENING WORTH IT?

You wonder as you stand there watering flowers because it is hot and dry and there hasn't been enough rain: is gardening worth it?

You look at the plants you thought you were taking good care of and find that once again some of them look crispy around the edges like you've never watered them before, and others look as limp as a pile of old, green rags. You ask yourself: is gardening worth it?

You go inside after just a few minutes in the garden dripping with sweat, with your arms covered in mosquito bites making you look like a kid who just got home from summer camp and ask: is gardening worth it?

You practically crawl into the house after lugging bags of mulch, spreading it around those flowers that can't seem to get enough water, your back aching and complaining, and wonder: is gardening worth it?

You avoid looking at some areas of the garden that are more weeds than plants you planted and hope no one sees the mess before you have a chance to weed again, and ask yourself: is gardening worth it?

And then you see it. A hummingbird is flitting from one flower to the next, grabbing all the nectar it can get. You stand still, as still as you can, and watch it for several minutes, not once thinking to reach for your smartphone so you can take a picture or video of it. It's a moment between just you and the hummingbird and it will stay that way. Yes, you decide, gardening *is* worth it.

You see all the bees buzzing around, covering themselves with pollen, and you know the answer is yes, gardening *is* worth it.

Then you pick a few leaves of lettuce sown in a container on the patio and grab a handful of just-ripened tomatoes to make a simple salad to go with the savory pie you made with some zucchini squash picked from your own garden. The answer is obvious with every bite. Yes, gardening *is* worth it.

Gardening is worth the sweat. It's worth the aches. It's worth the weeds. It's worth a few insect bites. It's worth the time to water, to plant, to harvest.

Gardening is worth it all.

ACKNOWLEDGEMENTS

Some people might look at the acknowledgements of a book as an afterthought, a place to list each and every person who in some way contributed to the writing, editing, and packaging of the book. It is that, but it is also like the compost pile in the garden. No one usually pays much attention to the compost pile when visiting a garden, but they should because the compost pile tells us a lot about the garden and how it came to be.

Here's the compost pile of this book, a place where there are a few more paragraphs you don't want to miss, a couple of final thoughts, and of course, some thanks.

Seeded and Sodded: Thoughts from a Gardening Life is the third book in a trilogy that started with my first book, *Potted and Pruned: Living a Gardening Life*, which was awarded the 2018 Gold Medal for Best Overall Book by GWA: The Association of Garden Communicators, now called GardenComm. The trilogy also includes my second book, *Homegrown and Handpicked: A Year in a Gardening Life*.

Thank you if you already own the first two books in this trilogy and have purchased this book to complete the set. Apologies to those who picked this book up first and now realize you have to get two more books to complete the set. Well, not really apologies, as I hope you want to read those first two books after reading this collection of essays.

As with the other books in my trilogy, there is a secret message in the chapter headings. Some people own the books for quite a while before they figure it out. Congratulations to you if you noticed right away. The graphics originally came from *The Garden's Story* by George H. Ellwanger (D. Appleton and Co., 1889), a book I found at a used book store.

I offer thank-yous to a few key people who have continued to assist me and encourage me in writing my books, including Deb Wiley, my content editor; Katie Elzer-Peters, my managing editor, and her team including copy editor Billie Brownell and the behind-the-scenes graphic artist Nathan Bauer. Thank you also to beta readers Sherry Weir and Cindy Tournier.

Finally, many thanks to countless supporters of all my writing efforts, including family, friends, and readers! Those efforts include my long-standing garden blog, *maydreamsgardens.com*, where many of these chapters took shape and form and where I virtually met many friends and gardeners who encouraged me and whom I now count as dear friends. Though I encourage everyone to leave the online world as much as possible and spend more time in their gardens, I still tip my hoe to that online world for enriching my gardening life.

ABOUT THE AUTHOR

Carol Michel is the author of *Potted and Pruned: Living a Gardening Life* (Gardenangelist Books, 2017), which received the 2018 Garden Media Gold Award for Best Overall Book from GWA: The Association of Garden Communicators (now GardenComm), *Homegrown and Handpicked: A Year in a Gardening Life* (Gardenangelist Books, 2018), and *The Christmas Cottontail: A Story for Gardeners of All Ages* (Gardenangelist Books, 2018). She is a lifelong gardener and resident of Indiana with a bachelor's degree in horticulture production from Purdue University. She spent over three decades making a living working in healthcare IT while making a life for herself in her garden. She is also an avid collector of old gardening books and claims to have the largest hoe collection in the world. A popular speaker for groups of all sizes, Carol has written for several magazines and regularly writes for her award-winning garden blog, *www.maydreamsgardens.com*.

LOOKING FOR A LITTLE MORE INFORMATION?

I continue to write posts for my blog, *maydreamsgardens.com*, and encourage you to subscribe to it so you don't miss a single post.

Like many gardeners and authors, I am also active on several social media outlets. Check out May Dreams Gardens on Facebook and Indygardener on Twitter and Instagram.

If you would like to listen to me talk about gardening, subscribe to my podcast, The Gardenangelists, recorded weekly with Dee Nash of *reddirtramblings.com*. You will find our podcast on iTunes, among other places, and you will find us as The Gardenangelists on Twitter, Facebook, and Instagram.

If you are interested in getting involved with other garden writers, please check out GardenComm, formerly GWA: The Association of Garden Communicators, *gardencomm.org*. If you think you would like to publish your own book about gardening or anything else, I recommend *thegardenofwords.com* as the place to start as you search for assistance.

If you are interested in meeting other gardeners in your local area, join or start a garden club. Hang out at your local garden center or greenhouse. Enroll in a Master Gardeners class offered by your local Cooperative Extension Service. Start your own garden blog and tell the world about your garden. Just don't stay behind your garden gate gardening alone.

And if you want to ask me something or just send me a note, feel free to email me at Indygardener@gmail.com.

www.ingramcontent.com/pod-product-compliance
Lightning Source LLC
LaVergne TN
LVHW021022250326
834688LV00016B/178/J